HEROES OF THE BIBLE

REMAINING FAITHFUL THROUGH YOUR LATER YEARS

10 Publishing
a division of 10 of those.com

First published in Great Britain in 2015

British Library Cataloguing in Publication Data

A record for this book is available from the British Library

ISBN: 978-1-910587-23-2

Designed by Diane Bainbridge

Printed in the UK

10Publishing, a division of 10ofthose.com
9D Centurion Court, Farington, Leyland, PR25 3UQ, England
Email: info@10ofthose.com
Website: www.10ofthose.com

Roger Hitchings

30 UNDATED DEVOTIONS

DAY 1

READ Genesis 15:1–7

Believing God

'Abram believed the LORD, and he credited it to him as righteousness' (Gen. 15:6).

Abram's faith in God was quite remarkable. He was a childless man of 75 and God promised that his descendants would be as many as the stars in the night sky, and he believed God! He ignored his advancing years and the growing limitations of his body. God had promised and that was enough for him. Such faith was the grounds of Abraham's acceptance with God as we are told in Genesis 15:6.

It is the same for us. The Apostle Paul reminds us in Romans 4:5 that 'to the man who does not work but trusts God who justifies the wicked, his faith is credited as righteousness'. So we believe that God justifies wicked people on the basis of Christ's death for sinners alone, without our contributing anything at all.

This is the glory of being a Christian. We depend entirely on what God has done for us through Jesus Christ. We don't depend on our own merits or efforts. We don't depend on our religious observance or some ceremony we have gone through. It is by grace alone, through faith alone, in Christ alone. Praise God for all His mercy and grace.

Abraham 'believed the LORD' and His promise despite his age and despite what his experience of life told him. It is so easy to listen to other voices than the Lord's. But when we do that we begin to rely on other things and not to depend entirely on Jesus Christ. Such thinking opens the door to doubts and uncertainty. Fears may come to us but we must simply look to Jesus. The fact is that, as justified sinners, we are completely accepted by God and there is nothing for us to add. No matter what our age we can trust in Him and know the glory of sins forgiven.

'Saved by grace alone! This is all my plea'

From the hymn 'Grace! 'tis a charming sound'

DAY 2

READ Genesis 18:1–15

Something to Laugh About

'Is anything too hard for the LORD?' (Gen. 18:14).

Sarah laughed when the Lord said, 'I will surely return to you about this time next year, and Sarah your wife will have a son' (v. 10). She couldn't help herself. The thought of having a child at 89 years of age seemed ludicrous. God had promised many years before that she would have a child, but it just hadn't happened. The idea that it would happen now was frankly incredible.

These three men had turned up, and one of them had made this extraordinary prediction. Sarah was caught off guard. It was too fantastic. But this was no ordinary visitor: it was the Lord of heaven and earth. He knew she had laughed. So he answered her unbelief with an even more astounding statement, 'Is anything too hard for the LORD?'

That had never occurred to Sarah. She knew a lot about Him because of His dealings with Abraham and herself over many years. But she had yet to learn that 'all things are possible' (Matt. 19:26; Mark 10:27) for this God who knows no limits.

If we are honest with ourselves we can easily feel like Sarah, especially in our later years. We have nursed hopes that the Lord might do certain things for us, but nothing has happened and we have given up hoping. We still trust the Lord, but there are clouds of uncertainty hovering at the back of our minds. And sometimes they trouble us and create a degree of despondency. But our God is the same as He was with Sarah. If He has promised, He is able to perform.

That is what Sarah found. One year later the baby was born. They called him Isaac at the Lord's instruction. Isaac means 'laughter'. (The Lord has a sense of humour.) 'Is anything too hard for the LORD?'

'The God of Abraham praise, who reigns enthroned above'

From the hymn of that name

READ Genesis 22:1–14

You Can Always Rely on Him

'God himself will provide the lamb for the burnt offering' (Gen. 22:8).

Abraham was 113 years old, and he was facing the greatest challenge of his life. God had told him to sacrifice his beloved son, Isaac. It was a puzzling command. God had promised Isaac, and now He was asking for that special child to be sacrificed. What a challenge! But God had commanded it and so Abraham obeyed. He trusted God implicitly. As Hebrews 11:19 tells us, he believed that God would raise Isaac from the dead.

When they got to Mount Moriah Isaac asked his father the poignant question, 'where is the lamb for the burnt offering?' (v. 7). That led to Abraham's wonderful response of faith: 'God himself will provide the lamb for the burnt offering'.

Abraham's response to Isaac was an illustration of his loving trust in God. Despite the awesome nature of God's command, he still rested on the faithfulness of God. That faith was honoured in the most marvellous way. Isaac was spared and a substitute was provided. It is a stirring and beautiful story.

Yet there was something else very special about what happened. Abraham and Isaac saw acted out before their eyes the great truth of Christ our substitute. They may not have understood it in those terms. But what they saw was that God provided a substitute. And that speaks of Jesus. Is that part of what the Lord was referring to when he said, 'Abraham rejoiced at the thought of seeing my day; he saw it and was glad' (John 8:56)?

Abraham named that place 'The LORD Will Provide' (v. 14) because he proved this truth in his greatest challenge. The Lord provides for our salvation, and He provides for our well-being in every part of life. You can always rely on Him whatever the difficulty because, through Jesus, the Lord always provides.

'Strength for today and bright hope for tomorrow'

From the hymn 'Great is Thy faithfulness'

DAY 4

READ Genesis 46:1–7

All May Change

'I am God, the God of your father ... I will go down to Egypt with you' (Gen. 46:3–4).

When we are old any change is unwelcome. We love things to stay as they are. We enjoy our comfort. In particular the thought of moving house and home can be just too much. Jacob felt like that.

Up until now Jacob had known all sorts of upheavals and turmoil through his life. But he had become settled in Canaan. And then a dreadful famine had come. He sent his sons to Egypt to get grain, but that turned out to be a disaster with Simeon ending up in prison. Then came the news that Joseph, who he thought had died years before, was alive and was in charge of everything in Egypt. And Joseph wanted his father to come down to Egypt so that he could look after him. Jacob knew he had to go, but he had considerable misgivings. He was 130 years old and taking such a journey was a challenge.

At the outset of this journey he came to Beersheba and he built an altar there to seek God. He received amazing comfort. The God of his father, Isaac, would not change no matter how circumstances changed. There was no need for anxiety and fear. Indeed God would go down into Egypt with Jacob. Everything was part of the divine purpose.

Changes may come to us and we may feel considerable anxiety and fear about them. Yet if God is in the change we must not refuse to comply. He who orders our days is the One who goes with us. That should give us courage and confidence. Let us say, 'The Lord is my helper; I will not be afraid' (Heb. 13:6). He goes with us, even into today, and we may be at peace. Let us fix our eyes on Him and not our changing circumstances.

'All may change, but Jesus never. Glory to His name!'

From the hymn 'Yesterday, today, forever'

READ Genesis 47:1–10

Blessings to Share

'Jacob blessed Pharaoh' (Gen. 47:7, 10).

This was a most fascinating conversation. You could hardly picture two more different people. Jacob was standing before mighty Pharaoh and answering his questions.

Jacob was a humble man, dressed in his shepherd's clothes. He had known many difficulties, failures and successes. He had come to Egypt because of his need and especially because God had sent him. And now he was facing Pharaoh, the greatest ruler on the earth at that time – someone with awesome power and resources, whose wealth was vast, as his court displayed.

Pharaoh asked him a strange question, 'How old are you?'(v. 8). It was not a disrespectful question; rather it was a way of showing honour. At 130 years of age Jacob was old, and clearly it showed. His life had been demanding. And yet Jacob admitted that compared to his father and grandfather his life had been short (v. 9; Abraham lived to be 175 and Isaac 180).

But age was not the greatest difference between the two. The biggest difference was that Jacob was able to bless Pharaoh both when he came in and again when he went out. And Jacob's blessing was of real spiritual value. Pharaoh could only give Jacob and his sons material things. He had nothing spiritual to impart. Jacob, on the other hand, knew God, walked with God and communed with God. He had something to give.

Years of knowing God, walking with God and communing with God give older people a treasure house of good things to share with others. As Psalm 92:14–15 says, 'They will still bear fruit in old age, they will stay fresh and green, proclaiming, "The LORD is upright; he is my Rock, and there is no wickedness in him."' How much you have to give today. What blessings there are to share.

'Such blessings from Thy gracious hand our humble prayers implore'

From the hymn 'O God of Bethel, by whose hand'

DAY 6

READ Genesis 49:8–12

Anticipating Jesus

'The sceptre will not depart from Judah' (Gen. 49:10).

Thinking about someone dying is not something most people enjoy. But Christians are different in so many ways and our approach to our last days is particularly distinctive. That is what we see in Jacob. His last seventeen years in Egypt were days when he was found blessing others – Pharaoh, Ephraim and Manasseh, and then his twelve sons. What a way to use your last days.

Here is the very last scene of his turbulent life. His sons were gathered around his death bed and he spoke to each of them (49:1–2). He was a man of God and a prophet. Each son was blessed in turn and for most of them Jacob's words had a sharp edge to them (49:3–7, 13–21, 27). But for Joseph it was a song of the mercies and goodness of God (49:22–26).

The greatest blessing, however, was reserved for Judah. It gives us one of the most profound and delightful pictures of the coming Saviour. He is presented to us as the rightful King and the Triumphant One. From this description comes the marvellous title 'the Lion of the tribe of Judah'. That title is used in the Revelation 5:5: 'the Lion of the tribe of Judah, the Root of David, has triumphed. He is able to open the scroll and its seven seals.'

To think of this magnificent description of our Saviour is to think the best thoughts. In the testings of old age, and even in that final test of death, we should be like Jacob and think of Jesus, the Lion of the tribe of Judah. Even today we may think on Him and take heart that He gives us the victory.

'For the Lion of Judah shall break every chain,

and give us the victory again and again.'

From the hymn 'The Lion of Judah'

DAY 7

READ Exodus 17:8–16

Better Together

'When Moses' hands grew tired ... Aaron and Hur held his hands up' (Ex. 17:12).

A group of older ladies sat together talking about their own usefulness as Christians and the gap there was in their church between them and the younger women. As they talked they came upon a solution. They decided to meet once a week to pray together for the younger women and to tell them what they were doing. As the younger women joined them, praying together became such a blessing for them all.

Moses learnt that. It was a critical moment in Israel's history. It was their first battle and the Amalekites they were facing were seasoned fighters. But Israel were God's people. While Joshua led the army, Moses climbed the mountain to pray. When Moses lifted up his hands to God in prayer, Israel were on top. But when his arms grew weary and dropped, then the Amalekites began to get the ascendancy. This problem was solved by Aaron (Moses' older brother) and Hur (his elderly cousin) coming alongside to help him. Three octogenarians were better together.

This was such a significant event that Moses erected an altar which he called 'The LORD is my Banner' because 'hands were lifted up to the throne of the LORD' (vv. 15–16). God exercised His authority but the prayers of three old men made all the difference.

In our later years we can feel that we are not very useful and that we can't make much of a difference. That is why it is good to do things with others and especially to pray together. Praying with others helps to keep our minds focused. We may meet together or by using a phone or email. What is important is praying together.

'The fellowship of kindred minds is like to that above.'

From the hymn 'Blest be the tie that binds'

READ Exodus 33:12–23

There is a Place

'There is a place near me where you may stand on a rock' (Ex. 33:21).

The incident of the Golden Calf is one of the most tragic in the Bible. The Lord's reaction to the wicked idolatry of Israel showed that. He said that he would destroy them and start again with Moses (32:9–10). What a dilemma for this great man. As leader he had constant problems with the people. He would agree with God that they were 'a stiff-necked people'. But he also had real concern for God's reputation.

As a result there follows one of the most wonderful examples of intercessory prayer as Moses pleaded with God for the children of Israel on the basis of God's honour and reputation (32:11–13). The Lord accepted His request (32:14) but said He would not go with them (33:3). Moses' response was in effect to say, 'if you don't go then I'm not going either' (33:14–15). His request for God's Presence was astonishing, but it clearly was the right thing to do because it was based on God's promise.

Yet Moses wanted more. He needed some assurance of God's favour. Perhaps he had been shaken by the fierceness of the Lord's reaction to Israel's sin. Whatever the reason he asked for something wonderful: 'Now show me your glory' (v. 18). And to this bold request he received a favourable answer: an answer to humble him by its privilege, to encourage him by God's grace, to strengthen him for the task that lay ahead, and to honour God who declared his name and glory.

At the heart of God's answer to Moses was a thrilling statement: 'There is a place near me' (v. 21). It is true for us as well. We may come with confidence to God (Heb. 4:16) and be bold in our requests. Moses set us an example that we may safely follow.

'There is a place of quiet rest, near to the heart of God'

From the hymn of that name

DAY 9

READ Deuteronomy 33:24–29

Strength for Today

'Your strength will equal your days' (Deut. 33:25).

How often do we start a day thinking to ourselves, 'I wonder how I will cope today?' Every day presents us with challenges and potential difficulties, but some days pose special threats and dangers. On such occasions we long for extra strength. Well here is a promise from the Lord to help us.

Moses was pronouncing his final blessing on each of the tribes of Israel. The last one was about Asher, and Moses said this tribe was most blessed. They would be kept safe and secure, and each day 'your strength will equal your days'. So whatever each day brought, there would be sufficient strength.

Then Moses added a general blessing on the whole nation. He explained all their – and our – blessings and why there was – and is – sufficient strength for each day: 'The eternal God is your refuge, and underneath are the everlasting arms' (v. 27). With such an attentive Father there can be no doubt about the supply of grace and strength. As Isaiah wrote, 'Even to your old age and grey hairs I am he, I am he who will sustain you. I have made you and I will carry you; I will sustain you and I will rescue you' (Is. 46:4). What a promise that is – He will carry us. How attentive He is to our needs.

Moses was 120 when he spoke these words to Asher and Israel. His life had been full of difficulties yet he could surely testify that each day he was given strength. This is something we all can prove. Reflect on your experience and how grace has always been sufficient for you, and then give thanks. Take this promise and pray over it as you face whatever today may bring.

'Strength for today and bright hope for tomorrow,

blessings all mine, with ten thousand beside!'

From the hymn 'Great is Thy faithfulness'

READ Joshua 23:1–14

All Fulfilled

'You know with all your heart and soul that not one of all the good promises the Lord *your God gave you has failed. Every promise has been fulfilled; not one has failed'* (Josh. 23:14).

Joshua was looking back. But he had a very special purpose for doing so. He was now an old man and had not long left in this world. He wanted to urge the nation's younger leaders to finish the work God had given them to do. So he reminded them of what God had commanded. And then he crowned his exhortation to them with this wonderful statement of encouragement.

Looking back can be dangerous. We can look back and make false comparisons with the present, something we should not do (Ecc. 7:10). We can also look back and revive memories that leave us sad and discontent. We can even look back and be filled with regret at mistakes made long ago. We can look back and be distracted from what we ought to be doing (Phil. 3:13–14).

But Joshua was doing what we all should seek to do as we get older. He was seeing that not one of God's promises had failed. It was as though he ticked off in his mind every promise God had made to the children of Israel, and how that promise had been fulfilled. Joshua's ministry was nearly at an end. He had served God faithfully and proved His grace and goodness through a myriad of different situations. And in everything he had found the Lord faithful. He then recalled that to encourage these men to continue to trust their God.

Surely this is something we can all do. And we can talk about it to other people to encourage and strengthen them: 'Every promise has been fulfilled; not one has failed!' It is one the great ministries of older people (Ps. 71:18–19).

'Great is Thy faithfulness, O God, my Father'

From the hymn of that name

DAY 11

READ Joshua 24:14–24

No Change

'But as for me and my household, we will serve the Lord*'* (Josh. 24:15).

Joshua was about 110 years old. He had called all the leaders together to share his final thoughts with them before he died and to renew their covenant with God. It must have been quite an emotional time. He reminded them of God's great faithfulness and challenged them to greater commitment. They still had much to do. Not least was to get rid of the false gods they still had with them (vv. 14, 23). They needed to come to terms with the inescapable fact that to follow God meant to separate from practices that God abhorred (vv. 19–20).

A major part of what Joshua said involved reminding them of his own consistency and commitment. He had been a most faithful servant of God and the people. To stimulate them and to express his undying devotion to the Lord he made this great statement: 'as for me and my household, we will serve the Lord'. Old he may be, weary he may be because of all the demands of a long and earnest life, but there was no change in his attitude. His commitment was undimmed despite the years and the tears.

There is a strong temptation in our later years to look for acceptance, and to compromise on important things to gain approval. But when we think of the Lord's loving kindness to us, surely our answer must be the same – no change. Let us determine to go on seeking to minister to others in whatever way we can while we still can. Let us not give up talking of all the Lord's goodness. Let us always encourage others by our love and commitment to Christ. How should we face the years of our later life? By being no-change Christians – just like Joshua.

'Sing, pray and swerve not from His ways, but do thine own part faithfully.'

From the hymn 'Leave God to order all thy ways'

He Has a Purpose for Us

'Then Naomi took the child, laid him in her lap and cared for him' (Ruth 4:16).

Was there ever a more proud and happy grandmother than Naomi? Becoming a grandparent is always something special, but for Naomi it was out of this world.

She would never have expected that when she returned to Israel after her years in Moab. She had left Bethlehem with her husband and two sons (1:1–2). Tragically all three had died in Moab (1:3–5). When she returned to Bethlehem only Ruth, her Moabitess daughter-in-law, was with her (1:4, 6, 16–18). The prospects of grandchildren were very remote.

She showed that in the way she spoke on her return: 'Don't call me Naomi ... Call me Mara' (1:20). Naomi means 'pleasant' whereas Mara means 'bitter'. As she reflected on all her losses she could only feel that life had turned bitter on her: 'the Almighty has made my life very bitter' (1:20). Negative thoughts filled her mind.

Later years can sometimes feel like that. We can look back and think of what might have been. The decisions made in earlier years didn't turn out as we had hoped. And our present situation seems unpromising. We can easily begin to be bitter.

But God had different things in mind for Naomi. His great eternal purposes were being worked out. In our verse we see her holding her grandson, Obed. When he grew up he would become the father of Jesse, who would be the father of David (4:17). And amazingly Ruth would feature in the genealogy of the Lord Jesus in the Gospel of Matthew (Matt. 1:5–6). How amazing are God's purposes.

This should really encourage us, especially on those days when regrets plague us. The Lord is gracious. He overrules our wrong decisions to bring about His purposes through us. And He does things that we never expect. His purposes for us will always be for good.

'Leave God to order all thy ways, and hope in Him whate'er betide'

From the hymn of that name

DAY 13

READ 1 Samuel 8:1–9

Sorrows Flood

'But when they said, "Give us a king to lead us," this displeased Samuel; so he prayed to the LORD' (1 Sam. 8:6).

Samuel was getting old and beginning to struggle, and everyone knew it. He had been a great leader in Israel, faithful in his service to God and to his nation. But now a new leader had to be found. It should have been one of his sons but their lives were unacceptable. He had taught them and they knew what was expected of them, but clearly their reckless lives showed that they did not care.

Samuel's grief is something many older Christians know. Our children do not walk with Him. We had such high hopes for them but they have been sadly disappointed. Our sorrow and anxiety is intense. Many believers throughout our land know sorrow's flood.

But what was worse was that Israel were rejecting God Himself. They wanted a king. That was too much for Samuel. Could the people not trust God to raise up a new leader? That was what He had done when Samuel replaced Eli. But no, they wanted to be like the nations around (8:20). After all God's goodness and wisdom towards them they made this sad request. There was only one thing that Samuel thought of doing in response – 'he prayed to the LORD.'

We too must pray. It seems almost trite to say something so obvious but it is important to do so. Unbelieving children may be your sorrow today. It is your privilege to copy Samuel and to beseech the Lord of heaven to save your children and those of fellow grieving believers. Other issues, including the state of our nation, may cause you deep sorrow and distress. But God hears prayers for that as well. Samuel is an encouragement to keep on praying. The Lord hears and does answer. Samuel lived to see David raised up by God.

'What a privilege to carry everything to God in prayer!'

From the hymn 'What a friend we have in Jesus'

DAY 14

READ 1 Samuel 12:18–25

An Unacceptable Sin

'As for me, far be it from me that I should sin against the LORD by failing to pray for you' (1 Sam. 12:23).

Samuel's life was impressive. He showed such amazing consistency and faithfulness. He was a great leader and an even greater man of prayer. It is a theme that recurs throughout his story, and especially his old age.

It was not always easy. There were problems in Israel: Saul was getting old and in these later years the people asked for a king . Poor Samuel was hurt. But the Lord told him to go along with their request (v. 22), even though the nation had rejected Him.

Samuel's role as leader of the nation was ended and in our verses he was making his final speech. It was a sad and very emotional day for him as he spoke to the people. God gave a most awesome demonstration of His displeasure with the people by sending thunder and rain, which served to make them realise how much they owed to Samuel. They made one final request of him: they pleaded with him not to stop praying for them. His response was impressive: 'As for me, far be it from me that I should sin against the LORD by failing to pray for you.'

We can take our example from Samuel. In our later years we have to cease roles we have long fulfilled. But we can still pray. The Lord's people desperately need older saints to make time to pray for them. We must never underestimate the importance and value of praying. We are not to nurse our grievances, or to be full of self-pity. Rather we are to pray more for our brothers and sisters. It is a very serious matter if we neglect our responsibility to pray for the Lord's people.

'Prayer makes the darkened cloud withdraw;
prayer climbs the ladder Jacob saw'

From the hymn of that name

DAY 15

READ 2 Samuel 15:30–37

Ready to Serve

'Hushai ... was there to meet him' (2 Sam. 15:32).

David had reached the lowest point of his life. His son Absalom had led a very sizeable rebellion against him and David was having to flee from Jerusalem (15:13–14). He knew a double heartache: the pain of a father whose son had broken his heart, and that of a king who was facing a rebellion. Then came further bad news: the brilliant young Ahithophel, David's counsellor, was now one of Absalom's advisors. He would give the shrewdest counsel.

At the top of the hill David met his old counsellor, Hushai. He was an old man and becoming frail. He had served his king well for so long. Now he wanted to go with David. But he would only slow them down. David had to be very blunt: 'If you go with me, you will be a burden to me' (v. 33). No-one, and especially an old man, wants to be a burden.

However, Hushai was still full of wisdom and insight. David thought of something he could still do. He was the only person who could counteract Ahithophel. So David asked him to go back to Jerusalem and serve him there. David had prayed previously for the Lord to 'turn Ahithophel's counsel into foolishness' (v. 31). Through Hushai the Lord answered this prayer. Hushai was taking a great risk in doing so but he was willing to serve, despite his age.

Older people can so often be the Lord's answer to other people's prayers. Experience brings wisdom, which is a mark of godly old age. In times of crisis or difficulty, opportunities may come to serve. The Lord may use us in special ways in our last days. We must make sure we are prepared. It may be a demanding challenge but, if the Lord's people need us, may we be found ready.

'I'm not ashamed to own my Lord, or to defend His cause.'

From the hymn of that name

DAY 16

READ 2 Samuel 19:31–39

Being Realistic

'I am now eighty years old. Can I tell the difference between what is good and what is not?' (2 Sam. 19:35).

Barzillai is not the best-known man in the Bible, but he is someone we can all learn some valuable lessons from. When Absalom rebelled and David had to leave Jerusalem, it was Barzillai, with others, who fed David and all who were with him. Although Barzillai was a very rich man, doing this was still a huge sacrifice, but he was prepared to make it to serve God.

Later on, when David was returning victoriously, he wanted Barzillai to go with him as a mark of his gratitude. Although this was a great honour, Barzillai graciously refused the privilege because he knew his limitations due to age and physical condition. He was realistic about what he could and could not do. There was no bitterness in what he said; rather he put the honour of men into the context of eternity. He had a higher priority than the praise of men. His eyes were fixed on heaven and so he could be realistic about what he should try to do on earth. He let someone else take his place.

The sort of approach Barzillai took is very unusual. Too often we want to court the acclaim of others. We look for significance and want to be taken notice of. But our later years are not designed to be like that. There is a place for seeing our growing limitations and withdrawing from the activities we have done to focus on more important issues. This is a counsel not for inactivity but for a change of priorities. In Paul's words from 2 Corinthians 4:18, 'we fix our eyes ... on what is unseen.' It's simply being realistic.

'E'en down to old age all My people shall prove

My sovereign, eternal, unchangeable love'

From the hymn 'How firm a foundation, ye saints of the Lord'

DAY 17

READ 2 Samuel 23:1–7

Our Last Days – Singing Days

'The oracle of David son of Jesse ... Israel's singer of songs' (2 Sam. 23:1).

David sang God's praises all his life. So he could call himself 'Israel's singer of songs'. And old age did not stop him singing.

In this his last song he concentrated on the wonderful themes of God's grace. First of all he recounted what the Lord had said to him. God's word had come to him in a very personal way on a number of occasions and here he recalled those words and relished them in his heart. In particular he remembered that precious time when the Lord had made the most wonderful promises to him (7:1–17). That covenant was 'arranged and secured in every part' (23:5).

His last days were singing days because of the amazing extent of God's grace to him. He had wonderful things to sing about.

But David's songs were not just down to his own skill, although God had gifted him in a remarkable way. The Lord had also guided and inspired him as he sang: 'The Spirit of the LORD spoke through me; his word was on my tongue' (v. 2).

And are we less blessed? You may not be a great poet, and you may not be an outstanding musician. If you are, thank God for His gifts. But if you are not, you have other gifts of equal value. However, there is one thing that applies to all who are truly born again: it is that the Spirit of God lives in us and works through us. Let us, therefore, seek His help that we may wisely use our gifts for as long as possible. And above all else let us sing until our final day about the amazing grace we have known.

> ***'Amazing grace! How sweet the sound***
>
> ***that saved a wretch like me!'***
>
> *From the hymn of that name*

READ 1 Kings 11:1–8

Hold on

'As Solomon grew old ... his heart was not fully devoted to the LORD his God' (1 Kgs. 11:4).

There are so many encouragements in the Bible for us as older believers. But there are also some very solemn warnings. Solomon in his old age is one. He lost his focus on God and fell into serious sin.

The trouble was he followed the ways of the nations around and accumulated many wives from them in disobedience to the Lord. They turned his heart even further from the Lord so that he began to indulge in their idolatry.

It was Solomon who had written, 'Above all else, guard your heart, for it is the wellspring of life' (Prov. 4:23). That was just what he did not do – 'his heart was not fully devoted to the LORD his God.' And so the Lord had to discipline and rebuke him (1 Kgs. 11:9–11). It was a sad way to end such a great and useful life.

What happened to Solomon is a serious warning for us to consider. Our hearts can easily be distracted. The cares of life, physical frailty and limitations, anxieties and worries can all divert our mind. Our hearts can grow cold towards the Lord. We have to strive to maintain our walk with God. We have to be alert to the dangers. It can be hard to be old and remain godly.

But in case we get too discouraged by what happened to Solomon, the Holy Spirit tells us: 'as the heart of David his father had been' (v. 4). David faced temptations and the attacks of the evil one, but in his heart he did 'follow the LORD completely' (v. 6). Our God gives strength to the weary and to those who hope in Him. David did that and he found grace to hold on to the Lord.

'Only thy restless heart keep still, and wait in cheerful hope'

From the hymn 'Leave God to order all thy ways'

DAY 19

READ 1 Chronicles 23:1–5

Do What You Can

'When David was old and full of years, he made his son Solomon king over Israel. He also gathered together all the leaders of Israel ...' (1 Chr. 23:1–2).

The time came for David to step down. He had served Israel as king for 40 years, but age and frailty meant the time had come to hand over. So he appointed Solomon to replace him. But he still had one great task to finish.

David had had this one great ambition in his life: he had wanted to build the temple for the honour of the Lord (2 Sam. 7:2, 5). But God had prevented him from fulfilling his hope and had said that Solomon, his offspring, would build it (2 Sam. 7:12–13). So David devoted his last days to finalising the plans for the building and organising the way worship should be carried out when it was built.

It takes wisdom and courage to know when it is time to stop and let someone else do the job. We can find it hard to accept the effects of age. We can still think we are doing things well and so refuse to hand over. It may be that such a decision is difficult because we love what we are doing and we still want to serve. On the other hand it can be pride. That is where honesty, courage and wisdom are needed.

It is doubtful that any of us will have such a grand project for our last days, but the principle applies to us. David was concerned about God's honour. So in his final days he looked forward and focused on the one thing he could do. That is a great attitude to cultivate – 'When you cannot do what you would, do what you can' (Philip Henry). The thing is to look forward and live each day for God's glory.

'There's a work for Jesus, ready at your hand,

'Tis a task the Master just for you has planned.'

From the hymn of that name

 READ 1 Chronicles 29:14–20

An Example Followed

'Then David said to the whole assembly, "Praise the LORD your God."' (1 Chr. 29:20).

It was David's last act and it was a noble one. He had designed the temple and now he was encouraging the whole nation to be involved by giving towards the building. It was to be a really magnificent building – 'this palatial structure is not for man but for the LORD God' (29:1).

David gave his personal wealth (29:3–4), and he invited everyone else to give too. The response was so extraordinary that everyone rejoiced (29:9). Then David led the people in a wonderful prayer of thanksgiving. And when he had prayed he called on everyone there to 'Praise the LORD' (v. 20).

David wanted the temple to be so impressive because he wanted to glorify God. So he set the people an example of generosity and worship and they followed. Of course, he was king and that influenced everyone. But the principle he applied is one that works throughout life.

One of the things the Bible teaches us is that older people are to be an example. Their conversation and conduct is to be such that others will want to emulate them (Tit. 2:2–5; Heb. 13:7). This happens most when we desire to honour God above everything else.

Too often we who are older can be full of complaints about what is happening in the world and in the church. That is not a biblical way to behave. We must face up to the reality of life with all its trials and troubles, but they should not dominate our thoughts. Rather we are to be those who praise the Lord from full hearts of love and we are to be generous in spirit. Then, by God's grace, we will give an example to be followed.

'Fill Thou my life, O Lord my God, in every part with praise.'

From the hymn of that name

DAY 21

READ Daniel 6:16–23

Faith Unfailing

'And when Daniel was lifted from the den, no wound was found on him, because he had trusted in his God' (Dan. 6:23).

There is probably no better known story than Daniel in the lions' den. But what people tend not to know is that Daniel was in his eighties when this happened. He was still serving God in the place where He had put him in his youth (1:3–6). Faithful and conscientious, he impressed the mighty Darius who wanted to make him Prime Minister (6:3). But there were others who despised Daniel's integrity and thoroughness. So they hatched their plot and Daniel became the victim (6:4–7). Things were all against him.

But Daniel was a man of faith. He maintained his life of prayer and did not try to hide his devotion to the Lord (6:10). He was ready to pay whatever price that might involve. So into the lions' den he went. But it was Darius who had a bad night's sleep. Next morning he returned to see if anything was left of poor old Daniel. He got such a surprise. Daniel was there completely unharmed. God had been faithful to his aged servant.

What a tremendous encouragement this story is. And it is so relevant to us in our later years. It is a great danger in old age to look for the easy way out, to compromise and avoid risk. Our opportunities for service may be very different from Daniel's and our physical capacity may be less. But his faithfulness to the Lord and his unfailing trust in God are encouragements to us. Do our lives reflect the godly values that others take notice of? Do we respond to adverse circumstances with faith, confidence and a calm contentment? Do we have that total trust in our God?

The Lord will keep us and strengthen us. May our faith be unfailing.

'For I will be with thee, thy troubles to bless,

and sanctify to thee thy deepest distress.'

From the hymn 'How firm a foundation'

 READ Luke 1:5–20

Never Despair

'Zechariah asked the angel, "How can I be sure of this? I am an old man and my wife is well on in years"' (Luke 1:18).

Zechariah and Elizabeth were a most godly couple. In many ways they were the sort of people we all wish we were. The only real problem for them was that they had no children and both of them were getting on in years. Yet this older couple were to play a very important role in the story of the Incarnation, as other older people do. God answered their prayers in a very surprising way.

They clearly had prayed much about being childless for quite a time, but nothing had happened. Indeed having to wait so long had led to Zechariah losing heart. But then when he least expected it, Gabriel appeared to him in the temple and promised the birth of a son.

It had been such a long wait. The same could be said about Abraham and Sarah. But, no doubt, Zechariah and Elizabeth didn't dare to compare themselves with them. However, the angel was very clear that their days of sadness and disappointment were to be changed into days of joy and delight (vv. 14–15). Zechariah's unjustified unbelief showed he had concluded it was now too late for them to have a child.

It was not long after that the angelic promise became reality (1:24–25). What a wonderful answer to prayer that was, and it came in their old age, the most unlikely time. This is a tremendous lesson for older people. You may have prayed over some things for so long, and now you are in your later years you perhaps think it is too late. Don't despair! The Lord delights to surprise us by His grace even in our later years.

'Begone unbelief, my Saviour is near,

and for my relief will surely appear'

From the hymn of that name

READ Luke 1:39–45

No Age Barriers

'When Elizabeth heard Mary's greeting, the baby leaped in her womb, and Elizabeth was filled with the Holy Spirit' (Luke 1:41).

Mary was facing a very demanding time. She was quite young and she was expecting a child by the mighty power of the Holy Spirit. The Lord understood her dilemma and Gabriel told her about her elderly relative, Elizabeth, being pregnant (1:36). Mary went straight off to visit her.

When she arrived at the house, there was this marvellous incident that is so full of encouragement for us all. Three wonderful things happened. First, the six-month-old foetus in Elizabeth's womb responded to the presence of Mary, and the recently conceived child in her womb, by leaping for joy – an extraordinary reaction. Then second, Elizabeth, filled with the Holy Spirit, brought the most profound words of encouragement to the young mother, directing her thoughts to the faithfulness of God (v. 45). Third, Mary responded with the most delightful words of praise to God, which we call the Magnificat.

They were two very unusual mothers – an old lady beyond childbearing age, and a young woman who was still a virgin. Both had proved what Gabriel had said: 'nothing is impossible with God' (1:37). And now they were encouraging and supporting each other. With God there are no age barriers.

It is such a lovely picture and one that should encourage us. This is also an example of a very important role for older people. Younger people need encouragement and help, and older people are ideally equipped to provide that. What is more, it is a role the Lord has prescribed for us – see Psalms 71:18; 145:4.

Being an encourager is a wonderful ministry. Let us think and pray today about how we might make an opportunity to get alongside someone younger than ourselves so that we might be an Elizabeth to them.

'Blest be the tie that binds
our hearts in Christian love'

From the hymn of that name

DAY 24

READ Luke 1:57–66

Needed Correction

'Immediately his mouth was opened ... and he began to speak, praising God' (Luke 1:64).

For nine long months Zechariah had been unable to speak. It must have been a great trial to him. His voice had been taken from him because he did not believe the message the angel Gabriel brought to him (1:20). So throughout the time of Elizabeth's pregnancy he had been silent. It appears he communicated by using a writing tablet, so conversations must have taken a long time, or been very brief. Even when the baby was born, his voice did not return. It was only when he named the child 'John' in obedience to the Lord's command that he was able to speak.

But the time of discipline had been a benefit to him. When his voice returned he did not express relief that it was all over, nor did he start talking about what it had been like to be silent for so long. As soon as his voice returned he began to praise the Lord (1:67–79). And what tremendous words of praise they were: so full of Christ and the wonderful purposes of God. Undoubtedly he had been meditating on such things, and now out of a full heart he expressed his praise.

I don't suppose we often think about the Lord's discipline in our old age. Of course, most of the difficulties we face are due to the effects of ageing and illness. But there are times when we grieve the Lord and He responds to us with His loving disciplines. We will know when such times are, and they are always for our benefit (Heb. 12:5–7). He is always working to make us more holy (Heb. 12:10–11). Zechariah was an old man but he profited from the discipline he received, and so may we. Let us praise God for all His varied mercies to us.

'More holiness give me, more strivings within. More patience in suffering, more sorrow for sin.'

From the hymn of that name

DAY 25

READ Luke 2:25–32

Seeing Salvation

'For my eyes have seen your salvation' (Luke 2:30).

Simeon is one of the great men in the Bible. We don't know much about him –we don't even know his age. He was probably an old man because once he had seen Jesus he was ready to die. What we do know is that he was a very godly man and God had told him he would not die until Christ was born. And so he waited and believed God's promise.

Then one day he felt an urging from the Spirit to go into the temple. There he saw an ordinary-looking couple with a baby. He went to them and he took the baby in his arms. He knew who that child was. He was the long-awaited Messiah, God's promised Saviour. Seeing this little boy was the culmination of his long life. He could die happily now.

This little baby boy was the hope of all men – 'a light for revelation to the Gentiles and for glory to [God's] people Israel' (v. 32). That thrilled his soul. But there was another side to the impact this child would have. He would grow up to divide men, to humble and to save many. And what would happen to Him would cause great grief to His mother. Salvation for sinners involved a cross of awesome shame and distress.

We reflect on this great old man's wonderful words of hope and we rejoice as he did. Most of us think about the end of our days, and as we do we take comfort and delight in the One who is our salvation. Thinking about Him, and seeing His love and sacrifice for us, brings joy into every situation we have to face, including our death.

'For yonder a light shines eternal,

which spreads through the valley of gloom'

From the hymn 'I saw a new vision of Jesus'

DAY 26

READ Luke 2:36–38

An Influence for Good

'Coming up to them at that very moment, she gave thanks to God and spoke about the child to all who were looking forward to the redemption of Jerusalem' (Luke 2:38).

How old was Anna? Commentators disagree on her exact age but all agree she was an old lady. More particularly she was a very godly old lady. She spent most of her waking day in the temple area praying and engaging with other true believers. And she knew all about Simeon and God's promise to him that he would not die until he had seen the promised Messiah. So when she saw Simeon talking to a young couple who had a baby, she was all attention. She joined in and heard the most amazing things about this baby.

Her reaction was twofold. First, she praised God. What else could she do? What Israel had longed for and what the world needed above all things was taking place. The Messiah had come. Her joy was unconfined. Jesus, the Saviour, was in the world; nothing would be the same again. So second, she rushed off to find everyone she knew who, like her, was waiting for the Messiah. And she spoke to them all, and no doubt anyone else who would listen, about the Saviour.

What is so lovely about Anna is that her delight in the good news about Jesus meant she praised God and spoke to others. Isn't that an encouragement to you? What can you do in your last years? You can praise Him. And then you can talk to others about Him. You don't have to be able to answer all the questions people throw at you. All you need to do is speak about how wonderful He is. Rejoicing and testifying older people are rare. But they are a mighty influence for good.

'Tell out, my soul, the greatness of the Lord!'

From the hymn of that name

A Surprising Argument

'I then, as Paul – an old man ... appeal to you for my son Onesimus' (Phlm. vv. 9–10).

Paul loved Onesimus. He had been a slave in the home of Paul's friend Philemon. But he had run away. That was a terrible crime (vv. 15–16). Paul had met him in Rome while he was in prison, and had been the means of his conversion (v. 10). The runaway slave had become a great blessing to the aged Apostle and a very close bond had grown up between them.

But Paul knew that he could not keep the young man with him. He had to send him back to Philemon. Yet he wanted his friend to treat this young man with love and tenderness (vv. 15–16). So he sent this message to him.

It is a moving appeal. But it is also a surprising one. Paul could have used his authority as an Apostle to command Philemon about what he should do. Philemon would have complied. Yet Paul used another argument based on love. He reminded him of two facts. First, that he was in prison for the Gospel, and that should have carried great weight. Second, that he was an old man, which should have evoked respect and deference. So using these two arguments he told Philemon what he wanted him to do, and his arguments were totally persuasive.

In our culture older people are often devalued and ignored. Their views and wisdom are given no place. That can even happen in some churches. Older people can react to this attitude by feeling discouraged and unwanted. But the Bible says older people matter to God. They are valuable to Him. That is why Paul referred to his advanced age, for as a godly man Philemon would show him the respect that God expects (Lev. 19:32). Take heart today: the Lord has a high regard for you.

'Even down to old age all My people shall prove
My sovereign, eternal, unchangeable love'

From the hymn 'How firm a foundation'

READ 2 Timothy 4:6–8

Finishing Strongly

I have fought the good fight, I have finished the race, I have kept the faith' (2 Tim. 4:7).

Charles Simeon was a vicar in Cambridge from 1783 to 1831. When he was getting old it was suggested to him that he should slow down a little. His response was to say that he wanted to finish 'running hard'. He wanted his last years to be fruitful years.

The Apostle Paul had the same attitude. At the end of his life, as he was anticipating his death, he could reflect, 'I have finished the race'. He looked back at the past with thankfulness and satisfaction, and he looked forward with great excitement. What lay ahead was a 'crown of righteousness'. The anticipation that filled his soul with joy is the blessing of 'all who have longed for his appearing'.

Many older people endure great pain and suffering in their last years through illness and disability, and even the loss of mental powers. It is only the reality of grace in our lives that enables us to look back with thankfulness, and to look forward with excitement. Whatever our condition in these final years, we can contemplate what is ahead and know that the future is bright.

By faith Paul saw what lay ahead and he found strength in its promise. He kept 'running hard' in his trust in God and in his living a holy life. He celebrated what God had done in his life in the past and he rejoiced in what God had in store for him in the future.

This is something we all should seek to do. May God give us courage and grace to look back with thankfulness, to look forward with joy and so to live in the present. Then we will be able to say we ran hard to the finishing line.

'Far off I see the goal; O Saviour, guide me'

From the hymn of that name

DAY 29

READ 2 Peter 1:10–15

Godly Remembrances

'I will always remind you of these things' (2 Pet. 1:12).

It is very easy to forget things that matter. Other things crowd our minds and divert us. The pressures of life make us focus on lesser things. Distractions come from so many quarters. For many of us age and frailty mean that we forget more easily. For some illness afflicts us and our memories become lost. We need to be reminded.

Thank God for men like Peter. Though old and not long for this world, he saw the importance of reminding believers about the essential truths of the gospel. The churches he was writing to faced very difficult times. It would have been easy for them to have been diverted from the main truths. They needed the wisdom of the elderly Apostle to keep them on the 'straight and narrow'.

All of us in our later years can become lax about the way we live and about our devotion to the truth. We can start to approve things that once we would have rejected. We need to be constantly reminding one another of gospel truths.

The gospel can so easily begin to be diminished by the influences of the age. Younger people can be so pressured by modern life that they do not notice what is happening. But we who are older have time to reflect, to discern the trends and to offer gentle and loving advice.

We must avoid constantly reminiscing about the past. That is unhelpful, as Ecclesiastes 7:10 warns us. But we can be remembrancers who thoughtfully keep the great truths in front of everyone's eyes. In our prayers and praises, and in our conversations, we can joyfully refer to the wonderful truths that have sustained us through the years. It is a great ministry.

'Here I raise me Ebenezer,

hither by Thy help I'm come'

From the hymn 'Come Thou fount of every blessing'

DAY 30

READ Revelation 1:9–16

Looking at the Right Things

'On the Lord's Day I was in the Spirit' (Rev. 1:10).

The book of Revelation was the last book of the Bible to be written. The Apostle John wrote it when he was in his early nineties. He was in exile on the prison island of Patmos. It was not a nice place to be, especially at his age. But he was there because he loved and served Jesus and had been banished as a result.

So there was John on that bleak island and it was Sunday, the Lord's Day. How could he worship the Lord in such circumstances? How could He praise the Lord when things were so difficult? Well, he could and he did – because his heart was fixed on the One who loved Him, and that put everything else into context.

He was 'in the Spirit' on that Sunday. He was spiritually awake and every part of his mind and soul was focused on the Saviour. He was in communion with Him and he was permitted to see and hear the most amazing things. But most of all He saw Jesus (vv. 12–18).

Sometimes hardships and sorrows come into our lives entirely because we love the Saviour. He is precious to us, and in being faithful to Him we experience opposition from other people and sometimes even from people we love. Just being old can also be a great trial, one of the greatest we have to face. But we still want to be faithful to the Lord.

What we need when we are old and facing the great challenges that come with age is to know the grace of God that helps us to focus on Jesus. Don't keep looking at your circumstances; seek the Lord and think about His word. Engage in communion with Him. It truly is our greatest comfort and blessing.

'Turn your eyes upon Jesus
look full in His wonderful face'

From the hymn of that name

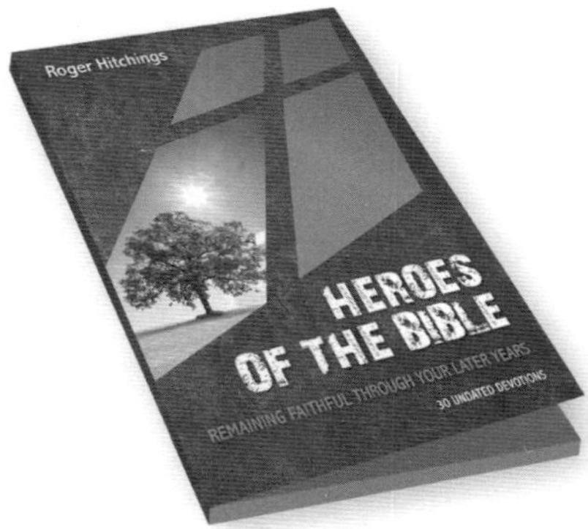
Roger Hitchings
HEROES OF THE BIBLE
REMAINING FAITHFUL THROUGH YOUR LATER YEARS
30 UNDATED DEVOTIONS